# STARDUST
## FOR BREAKFAST

ana m. s. smith

*For Michael, Rosalee, and Tabitha,*
*and mostly for myself.*

**s t a r d u s t**
**/ (ˈs t ɑ ː ˌd ʌ s t) /**

---

*noun*
dusty material found between the stars
a large number of distant stars appearing to the observer as a cloud
of dust
a dreamy romantic or sentimental quality or feeling

## 93 PERCENT STARDUST
We have calcium in our bones,
Iron in our veins,
Carbon in our souls,
And nitrogen in our brains.
93 percent stardust,
With souls made of flames,
We are all just stars
That have people names.
### -NIKITA GILL

"The cosmos is within us. We are made of
star-stuff. We are a way for the universe to know itself."
### -CARL SAGAN

# Table of Contents

## PART TWO: INSIGHT

*Part One:*
# UNREQUITED

## Thread of Hope

Those eyes possess me, though I,
In my human nature,
Try not to stare too hard into your soul.
Your hands, aware and arousing,
Bring me to life. I want their touch forever,
Upon my no-longer-motionless body.
Soft and full, I lust after lips
Never touched by another. Mine alone.
Secrets divulged to you, stay kept. My heart,
It beats against your chest, and you can feel its rhythm.
"Wait, wait, wait."
And so we stop for now,
Still never having sealed each other
Away with a kiss.

## AB1

silent drops
of sunlight
speckle the hard,
cold, grass;
the perfect, cloudless
blue sky
reminds me
of California.
and yet the best
of me fears a
reluctant return, or
none at all,
and so come the tears.

## Atomic Cornflakes

Reaching out like a sacred writing,
My heart to yours–
Stealthily hidden in abundance of
Laughter, with its fleshy undertones–
Nervous surrender
To a true dream.
Every time I think, a bombardment
Of emotional turmoil upheaves.
Hamlet's ocean of moral ills
Seem not to compare
To my undying, romance-hearted
Soul.
I hate frustration.
Simple, beautiful blue eyes
Penetrate and burn my heart,
My mind.
Intellect, rotten from passion;
Logic committed suicide long ago.
Oh, so far away in my waning light
I see a future shattered and
Glued back together–
Super-glued, gray-green glass
Of my woeful happiness.
Dried up, crisp pieces of black
Paper,
Ashes of my destiny,
Ensure the viewer of my once-fiery
Existence,
And what a beautiful coffee table it was.

**Boys**

Broken, bobbing heads,
All wanting kisses,
And me, just out of their reach.
Silly, far-fetched dreads
Form in my waning consciousness
About doubts and fears and falling in love.
There is some dim light shining
From the ones
Who tell you they want the truth,
And nothing but the truth,
From you,
But really they just want you to like them.
I'm just zipping through,
In this cynical and naked light.
I don't stand a chance.
Break their heart, and break my own–
Pieces drop off and shatter
On the sidewalk–
Cement heart, from loss,
Dreams and standards too high
To even be considered a drug anymore.
Small, wet, slimy feelings:
Delusions of what could be, eventually.
And what else is there?

## My Dear Sir

I see it in the way you smile.
The subtle undertones of something more obscure,
Something more obtuse.
I see it in the tune of your laughter,
The sound your breath makes when you sigh,
The depth of reason,
The incomprehensibility of your groveling nature.
I don't deserve this wonderful insurrection of will
But I love it.
I love you for advertising that to me.
I see in you: hope, truth, love.
I can see our house, our beautiful children.
Seeing through the illusions is like looking at a mirror;
An image appears,
And although you may not like it,
It's there, and it's yours to keep.
I want to see you there.

## The Tones of You

You ravished my soul with a word.
Your voice melted any insecurity
With its sympathetic, sweet cadence.
The depth of intense reason,
And the cover a single kind phrase brings,
Draw me towards your matchless
Sensibility.
The pitch of your unequaled inflection
Pulls me inward to your grasp.
There, in your embrace, I can hear all the world
At our fingertips.
The tenor from which you evoke laughter
Makes me tingle with giddiness–
Unable to hide my own exuberance.
You make me happy.

**Involvement**

Reluctant to give
But ready to Relinquish:
I send you my love
And walk away.
I miss you.
I hate you.
I want to confess
That sometimes you are on my Heart.
Solitude that bites
Cold, throbbing in my chest,
A hidden relic of the once-passionate,
Once-happy, once-new,
Life.
Now only a glimmer,
A faint, dim hope
Of what is to come.
Reconciliation:
A word I can't come to terms with.
Should we ceasefire?
It seems already something
Has been Settled.
The reunion seemed to be a Resolution
And yet a channel of Revulsion
And Springs of Distaste unearth Bitterness;
It still is there.
It never goes Away.

## Te Adoro

I wish I could turn my ring inside out
So people could see the inside–
The side that no one's supposed to get to see, but I do.
This side is opposite "the pretty side," the hidden side.
It's the side that touches me all day; the unpolished side.
This side tells the quality—the value—of the ring.
The grandeur of its simplicity is rare,
A thing seldom supplied
and a thing taken for granted all too often.
You are my encircling thing.

## Unsure, Yet Expectant

The shadows of my self-consciousness
Slightly ease away.
Like a stranded dog with its tail between its legs,
I run from the strange and undone,
But trust a gentle touch,
If you can catch me.
In the midst of the liquid pulse of life,
Rising and falling in placidity,
I find rest and open peace
In the face of my Unseen.

## Eilatan

I thought you would have the decency
To introduce her to me yourself.
You cheat.
Why didn't you tell me instead of making me wait?
I know this is all part of your very distinct blueprint plan.
I know I wasn't.
It upsets me that you wasted me.
I can't believe how heartless you really are.
She's lovely. You don't deserve her.
She's smart and pretty and petite–
Just what you wanted.
My wish is that you would be completely honest with her.
Does she know about me at all?
Or will that always be something
Remaining in darkness?

Do me a favor, and go rot.
Congratulations.

## Graduated Unpeace

I am craving conversation,
Not getting any–
Creating emphasis and mediocre speech
From sheer power of disrupted thought.
I want a reprieve from life,
From concentrated, bottled energy
To sleek, beautiful, jeweled, chaotic unrestraint
For once.
Dysfunctional spasms of happy-go-lucky
Aren't enough anymore.
Unfiltered entry I wish upon myself–
To know nothing and everything altogether.
Can I do that?
Please?
So obvious I must've missed it–
Top secret: unreliability.
Don't tell anyone.
I will take this slow churning in stride,
And let myself be insane for a while–
The summer at least.

**Emergency Ice Cream**
*in honor of George Malcolm Vinson Sr.*
*and Philip John Cornell*

You had an awake day.
The day was gently thrust in your direction;
I wondered if it would be good all day.
An old man introduced himself to me.
He's known me forever.
I got him milk more than once.
"I miss my bottom teeth!"
He said.
And it was a good day;
Full of gritty disrespect,
Rain, Mexican dominoes,
Good steak (How can vegetarians exist?),
And dancing to your own beat
In a golden-lit downpour.
Paltry, sultry, wang-nuttiness at your door.
I'm always waiting for the real moments–
They kick in,
Things happen
When you're awake.

**Early**

In this pink daylight of a morning
I sit and pray, and extinguish
Any thoughts or hopes of unrighteous
Exposure to the person who makes me
Laugh.
In this bright presence, I feel that same
Small stir that got me here to begin with;
A shock's in store—I can tell—and
Memories of the faintest caverns in my
Body being some kind of touched arise.
In this unreasonable, undecided hour of
Heart-truth awakeness I advance
In the starlight of something I didn't think
I was still angry over.
In this clean, dawning moment I make
Amends and break the ones that haven't yet
Been made. It is still too soon.

## Velcro Search and Rescue

The stiff, stifling shift
Of sands passing through
The eye of unreasoned loss
Make me think upon
A certain someone
And count *his* losses.
My undeserving unreservedness
Will never beat for him again.
The absence of an absolute,
Coherent definition of relations
Always bothered me.
And the upside is
Not just my fragmented dream
Shredded,
But I didn't do anything
Stupid; just like he asked.
I'll go after someone
Who'll chase me,
Someone happy, with me.

## Guardian of My Heartless Endeavor

The unlimited squalor of you
And your incapacity for sweetness
Makes me crazy with compassionate folly
And makes me feel bitterly rejected.

I read a poem once
Of a man who was the same way.
He made me feel how he felt,
And determine never to be like that.
So here I am now,
Feeling this way, acting like a starving artist:
Loathing my ingratitude, my fixed cunning,
And my wild ignorance.
As spiders weave,
As waters flow,
As men disagree,
And as life itself is revolving
Around its center,
I sit, dumbfounded by you.

## Holding it Together

Holding it together
Just until I see you
Then there are tears
And falling
And the struggle
Reality hits
Hard
Salty sadness
Dripping anxiety
Muffled suffocation

**Close By**

Will you let me look?
Your dark hair and piercing eyes
Draw me in.
Draw me into your arms.

Paint me into your life.
I'll be your illustration,
Your favorite rare beauty,
Hidden away for a while.
Shaped, by decree,
Into a masterpiece.
I'll be yours.

## Benediction

Sidewalk graffiti
Anointed by honeysuckle;
I pass by
This hot row of
Churches–
Scorched,
Overheated,
Fried,
And tried.
The end of normal pine trees
And the beginning of
A cloudless monsoon.
I pray
And walk.
The same bloodshot
Park bench
Beckons me be seated.
But that altar
Is too dangerous.
I kneel,
Buckled over
Only when the pain
Is too hard to bear.

**Pudding People**

"I don't drink flavored coffee." she said.
I thought to myself: There is no reason not to.
I think she just wants to be considered
Unique and different.
But then again, who doesn't?
Her sidekick always wants
To find a point of contention too;
Seemingly so sweet, and yet always lurking
In the corners of your mind, digging around.
Just be friends.
Just laugh
When you all find something
Funny together.
The point isn't to argue
Over things you don't agree on.

## The Cinnamon-Roll-Like-Biscuits Evening

Front-porched out with Tina's niece–
We weathered the "storm" side by side–
I hear the voice of a singing red-head
And know that I must return.

California rain just isn't the same,
But I'll take what I can get.
The scent doesn't change in those first bright drops,
For a minute I had no qualms.

Quiet flour and no cream of tartar
That was the afternoon that it was.
Sanctified, and wanting it; Quilted in love:
Which explains everything in my heart.
Rainy moments, while storming asleep,
Kept only slightly hidden in palm tree seclusion,
Cause my sentiment to settle, my will to change,
And a surrender to the knitting way of life.

## Enlisted

Not knowing much of anything,
Feeling utterly bewildered for much of the
first month,
We finally all met, for real.
Nervously determining to stay closed to this group,
And finding out these are the only ones
Who you know how to fight with properly.
The battles don't wait for you to be ready.
And you ARE the back-up when so many say
this is a waste.
They don't know that if it isn't for us
They will be dead forever.

So we go through the drills;
We practice the fighting;
Firsthand past wars always hindering
How we learn:
We need one thing.
The metal plates, artificial limbs,
Broken lungs, and sighing souls
Are mended with a new, better lifeline.
We sing some, we lose some.
But the fighting never stops.

How could you ever get empty?
I know you forgot about me
While you were in this place–
Not sure how though.
You made me into a tough-skinned
Piece of hot-wired, energetic, boiled ungirl.
I don't know how to put it.

I'm not so angry anymore,
But there's still a pocket
Of something somewhat putrid
That needs to burst somehow.
The summation:
You made me cry, and I wanted the idea of you.
You left and my mind stayed, my heart stayed.
When you visited you must've gone against
Every fiber of your conscience.
Didn't everything say no?
You involved another real, alive person
In your fleshly endeavor.
Did I start it? Well, I know I ended it too.
So is it all my fault?
I hadn't had the training.
I hadn't signed up for the army.
Didn't you know better than to take advantage of me?

You conducted yourself like a beast.
A small, fiery, uncontrollable, unready,
Pouncing, fondling, touchy-feely,
Hypocrite
Beast.
So I am here now.
And it makes me not trust.
And I don't know what to do.
And so I start a lot of sentences with "And,"
And call it a poem.

Something of me has to die to burst,
And you won't get the liquid spew in your direction at all
So it doesn't seem worth it.

Am I here to spite you?
I don't want to be.

## YP-CIA

People trapped in a mind
Gather,
So young,
Pretending to be so old, stuck in their little bodies,
Going through the motions,
Trying to figure out who they are.
Enunciating properly, defining their style,
Declaring lines emphatically, being cool,
Thinking they are fooling us:
Making the right faces,
Praying the right prayers
With their eyes closed and
Their heads tilted the right direction.
As if that's what we believe.

Yet still goofing off,
Speaking Korean,
Making faces across the room,
Practicing talking with their eyes.
I want it to be real so bad.
I see most of them
Once a week–
Maybe I don't even know their names,
All of them–
But some deep desire burns a hole
Through my heart
For them.
I don't want to be fickle.
They need me desperately to stay

And be real and normal.
I want to slap some of them,
My heart is filled with love
And strong prayers,
And shaking my fist at the Devil.

## Church

I don't know how
I didn't see it before.
You made your mark,
All I did is ignore
The warning signs
Of a million red flags;
You shut me down,
And had the gall to brag.
I was a cog in that machine
Called "Do it right,
And never be seen,
Do it my way,
Hide your tears,
Sweep it under the rug,
Don't voice your fears."
But I was was born to rise,
I was born to fly.
You tried to trap my heart
In continual lies,
A victim to this cruel system
Of errors and misguided disguise.
Always running,
Chasing a distant prize;
Waiting for a future
That never would come,
Dying for true friends,
Who can share their love.
Starving for affection, and
Knowing there's more to life

Than just spinning my wheels,
And hoping to die.
I found a new love song,
I'm drinking in peace.
I've discovered a sanctuary
Filled with relief.
Through the death of some dreams,
Through unbearable grief
Came bursting forth paths
Which brought me back to belief.
I may never know
All the answers in life,
But right here and right now,
I step out of this fight.
I'm resigned to the fact
That you won't understand
How I could derail,
Reject all you had planned.
In my heart, I still love you,
I believe we can mend
If we meet in the middle
Quit playing pretend.
I'm done seeking approval,
Finished living in fear.
You must decide for yourself
If you need me– I'll be here.

## TREmBLInG

You are like water in the sky:
You brood in the clouds,
Forming, and mulling,
Blown about by different winds,
Then an outburst, an expression,
A pouring out, a deluge:
Sometimes icy pellets,
Pounding down hard and cold and mean,
Cutting edges in your eyes, stabbing,
Hurtful, traumatized, reacting to a past season.
Unbroken floods of doubt,
Making rivers of self-consciousness,
Puddles of hopelessness.
Sometimes silently dripping down the window
Calm, even, constant– this I know–
Masking the world in sympathy and sadness,
Ever-washing, never-stopping,
Pity and woundedness and insecurity.
Sometimes a drizzle
I want to walk in,
Droplets gathering on my eyelashes,
Making my hair sparkle in the gray light–
Even though we can't see the sun–
Finding all kinds of wildlife nurtured,
At ease,
Glazing the world with reflective peace,
Self-aware, upturned, optimistic.
Sometimes frozen, white-faced, staring
Into the distance,
Frosted stillness, quiet.

Then crunching underfoot,
Indented under footprints of ancient heaviness–
Taking forever to melt.
But sometimes, sometimes
The light comes through you,
And a vibrant arch of color emerges,
Vivid just for a moment, volant,
Then gone.
Please, please, let in the light.
Be brave enough to face the sun.
Let the gathering of storm-clouds,
And the currents of imbalance
Disperse.
Move on into the brightness.

**Broken**

Sharp edges and
Broken, metallic
Voices
Echo in the
Amplification of my
Own inward yelling–
"I can't do this anymore."
"I don't deserve you."
"I have nothing left to give."
My heart is
A minefield of
Silent weaponry–
Aching, burning,
Hidden and undisclosed
Explosions lying
In wait.
How do I know when to leave?
Where is the confirmation
That things will never change?
There is confirmation
In your sleeping in,
In your bathroom floor briefs,
In your never answering those texts.
There is confirmation
In your frozen dismissal of my statement,
In your ignoring my words,
In your countless inactions.
I can't be this naïve.
Not still.
Not after nine and a half years.

How blinded I have been
By the trying to help you grow,
By the attempting to be a bigger person,
By the being your best friend,
But you never being mine.
I love you,
And it's not fair for me to stay
Here
Abusing you like I have.
It's not fair to you for me to
Go through life as your roommate,
Never opening up,
Never allowing you to comfort me,
Never trusting you,
Never respecting you,
Never valuing your expertise.
It's not fair to you for me to
Use your money,
Critique your parenting,
Correct your grammar,
Keep doing things for you
Instead of letting you learn how
To be a man.
We both need to explore,
Learn,
Grow up,
Find faith,
Find healing,
Find home.

# Part Two:
# INSIGHT

**Pancakes**

To proclaim adulthood
In the midst of
Anxiety
and
Major
Depressive Disorder
Reading about
Codependency
Might be a bit
Stupid
But this is the
Path
I am taking
I'm out
I can't stay here
Wallowing in self-pity
I have to
Do something
Say something
Care
Fight for my life
Live
Eat pancakes
Find joy
Follow it home

**Telling**

You already knew,
But now you can
Begin the grieving.
I'm sorry
We didn't work,
I'm sorry
You have to deal
With this too,
I'm sorry
You're hurting.
This is going to be
Better, though.
We're going to be happier.
You'll get a complete,
Whole,
Healing,
Growing,
Fully alive
Mama,
And you'll know, then,
It is worth it
To chase
The life
Your soul requires–
The life of peace.
It's telling
That you commented
On my wiseness

When we snuggled
Before you
Slept.
These fairy hairs
Are going to be magical
For us,
I just know it.

**Exposed**

My heart
Is an exposed nerve–
Crackling,
Electric pain
Embodied
In a still-beating
Anomaly.
Fiery tears
Roll down,
Their path tattooing
Charred, scarred
Ravines
Into my cheeks,
And a lake of coals
Against my chin,
Before dripping off,
Re-opening my chest wound,
And flickering
Painstakingly-slowly
Toward freedom.
Look at it.
Look there.
Live free or die.

**Unlisted**

Salad
Nuts
Coffee
Bath towels
Hand soap
Detergent
Air freshener
Milk
Fuck
Fuck
Fuck
Why did I let you choose for me?
I'm standing here roaming
Like an idiot,
Not knowing what kind of everything
I prefer.
When did I disappear?
You didn't even notice.
Neither did I until just now,
Paralyzed,
Unknowing
How to grocery shop
For myself.

## Nuance

You are a deep, moving river,
You are to be explored:
Your trauma stones
At the bottom,
Lodged in that muddy
Childhood,
Occupied and empty caves,
The dry places
Where you barely made it through,
Unplanned disturbances,
Places where your waters
Are turbulent, twisting,
Whirlpools,
Shallow places.
You have unearthed treasure,
Beautiful creatures,
And unsung microbial baptisms.
Have you ever seen yourself
From within?
From below?
Have you seen the dazzling sunlight
On your surface?
Do you know how well you reflect
When you are calm?
Even if the movement is too slow,
Even if you think that place is too dark,
I want to know you there—
Endlessly turning over rocks,
Upsetting the sediment,

Finding a way to help it settle,
Finding the tragedies
And making them
Rest,
Planting beauty there,
Recognizing that
The algae-pain
Is there to feed
The flow.
Your majesty is
Enamoring,
Your current, overwhelming;
You smell like fresh air,
And you house boundless
Joy and depth.
You are an adventure,
A place to relax,
To float,
To find nourishment,
Belonging,
A sense of self,
A renewal of strength
And vigor,
And deep, deep love.

**Skin on Skin**

Everywhere we touch,
I feel the flame of you.
Not just body heat,
(Though that is there as well)
But this diamondfire-like energy,
Pulsating between us:
Skin on skin.
One sock on,
Finding joy in your joy,
Blinded by white sparks:
Skin on skin.
Shivering, and still balmy,
Awakening and relaxing
Simultaneously.
Desire burns
Always:
Skin on skin.
Rapt, enamored,
Drawn in, and bonded,
Hopeful and respondent:
Skin on skin.

## With You

Nearing extinction,
Vast blue
Understanding
Enveloped in insurmountable peace,
We try to make it effable.
Aching through the outright
Bright whiteness,
Unlocked belly laughter.
Falling—
Falling hard—
Holding on tightly.
Held and healthy,
We are inking this
Clairvoyance.
We have to try.
Free.
Whole.
True.

## (W)hole

Displaced dirt:
Lower me,
Freeze me.
Aching arms:
Betray me,
Buckle.
Throbbing fingertips:
Claw at earth,
Reach the edge.

Forever:
I could lower a rope or tree branch,
Or find something useful to do.

## Before We Kiss

attentive questions
disarming answers
pulling me up
pouring honey on a wound
healing power
drawing strength
no poison
happy butterflies
embraced security
holding my face
dissolving our anxiety
warm gold
brandished tears
no fear
intentional touch
pure ointment
opening my soul
letting you in
electric breaths
consenting heartbeats
no hesitation

# Part Three:
# IRREVOCABLE

**Sunny Side Up**

Resigned
In the very best
Happiest
Most self-aware
And beautiful surrender
To an unknown
Future.
I'm hopeful
For the first time
In a long time.

## Hunny Bunny

I bought new underwear,
Even though I know you
Won't see them
Because you have respect
For the boundaries
We set.
There's something about you
That makes me want
New nylon on my most
Vulnerable and intimate places.
You require that level
Of self-awareness
And commitment,
And you match it
With your own growth
And planning
And breath.
I anticipate my lips on you,
And my hand in yours
And whimsy, and laughter,
And depth and breadth
And exploration
Unknown to me before.
It takes my breath away,
Leaving me nearly speechless,
But never voiceless
(An important distinction).
How do you smell?
How does your body feel

Hugged against mine?
What does your beard feel like?
I know already that your eyes
And mind
And smile
And words
Sweep me away.
Smitten is the right word,
But it needs an amplifier.

## Heavy Lifting

Stones fall away
At least one more each day
I know you.
Today is fear
Falling away
And releasing me
Buoying upward
Into precious
Priceless
Peaceful acceptance
And utter belonging,
Uninhibited safety
In your heart of hearts.

I cannot wait until
I can feel your
Skin on my skin again,
And your touch,
And your hair,
And rememorize your gaze–
Your irises and pupils,
And to inhale whatever you exhale.
Life?
Newness?

Everything.
You are everything.

## Sing Song

I want to call you my love,
But we haven't said that
To each other,
Not yet.
And so I will continue
Just thinking "my love"
At the end
Of most of my sentences,
And waiting for
The right moment.

## Light

You are light,
And yet not blinding
Or too hot
Or noisy;
You're like the early
Pink sunrise
Over my peaceful, silent coffee–
Or like a bright orange sphere
I can't look away from,
Encompassed by
Aesthetically beautiful clouds.
You are like a warm, golden-hour glow
At the end of a rainstorm,
Piercing through the storminess
And reflecting, shiny,
Highlighting the cleansed surfaces.
You're the white light,
Darting and dipping
Over choppy waves on a windy day,
Dancing in open air.

Every aspect of you has been a
Deliberate edging out darkness
For me,
A movement forward
And upward.

I love that.
I love this.

## Peace

You smile
And my whole heart
Melts into easy affection.
Relaxation, and fearless wonder
Come on strong,
Bursting forth from
Melodies of wrinkles
At the edges of your eyes.
And I could drink
All you are
In your lighting up
The cloudy
Or lonely
Or unassured
Shadows in my mind.

## Intrepid

You are not afraid
For you exude strength.
My fears are assuaged
Because of this,
Because of you.
In your arms,
In your bed,
My body pressed to yours
Feels safe, always.
Even as I shed tears
Triggered from past selves,
Past memories,
Passed opportunities,
Salted speckles on your
Strong shoulders,
You don't mind.
You soothe me,
You pick me up
Like the weight of me
Is never too much–
Could never be too much–
For you.
For you are as steady,
Burning strong,
As the low orange sun,
Morning by morning.
And even as the moonless, silken sky
Has stars,
You are dotting my future

With sparkling light, and beauty,
I no longer ache to be and feel
Seen,
And the power in that
Is the most satisfying feeling,
Ever.

**Triggers**

Prickly kisses on my neck,
Your breath, deep and hot
In the hollow made between
Our close bodies,
And my fingers
Wrapped in your hair;
These are the magic,
The sinking in,
The dome of love-madness
Giving me chill-bumps
On my extremities.
Your fingertips find the creases
Where my hips meet
My back,
And roam up my spine.
I remind myself what you feel
When you touch me,
Pushing back the natural
Exposure of raw nerve endings
Anxiously flaring up,
Lying to me from their
Past life cave.
Fuck you, brain;
I fight for the present;
Learning good touch,
And support,
And love.

**Free**

No longer missing
Intimacy
Leaning in
Pulling back
Don't let me slip
Deliberate kisses
With shaky breath
Every single soft touch
Soothes another cut
My jagged edges
Fitting together
Now
Hot tears
In the wake of love
Given freely
Vulnerability exhumed,
Welcomed
And nurtured
Unusual
But kind
And safe

**Terms of Endearment**

You call me love
As if it's my name
As if it's me
And to you I am
Love
And you are mine
My love
I've never known
A love like this
A love that's me
A love that's my name
And a reminder
Of how my heart
Can ache in a good way
Wholly rapt
And mouth agape with the
Weightiness
And weightlessness
Of being love to you
And you to me

## Abiding

The inability to be vulnerable,
The tears that didn't matter:
Those are things of the past.

Being seen as I am,
Being valued and loved:
These leave me standing aghast.

You are holding me close,
You are building me up:
This is love that's designed to last.

**Over-Easy**

I wake up excited.
Spending days
And nights
Together is my favorite
Thing to do.
Defenses are falling.
I gear up for a fight
And end up feeling
Loved and known
And at ease.

## Buried Alive

I never much liked
Sleeping with another human–
Even sleepovers as a kid
Always felt crowded.
But I have always found comfort
The dimmer the light gets,
Secrets feel easier to reveal
In candlelit rooms;
It's easier to be vulnerable
In the dark.
Sleeping with you,
Having you know me
In darkness
And in light,
In peace
And in chaos,
Anxiety riding hard,
Is causing to grow
This seed of power,
Blossoming love.
Yes, it needs the light,
But it is rooted in
Those darknesses
Which often go unnoticed,
But which are
Sleeping pleasantly now.

## Yours

In the mess
Of my
Woundedness,
I can see
How much
You love
All of me–
The sharpness,
Even the foul things
Lurking
Beneath the depths,
Secreted away false narratives,
Intelligence that
I've decided is a sham,
Design that
I've determined
To be purely cultural,
The things always intruding
On my surety–
Me, balking,
Dragging against
The rough and cutting
Edges of my sanity,
Aching through the
Chaotic tangle
Of unrested,
Arresting past selves,
Groping for your hip
In the night,

An anchor to me,
A warmth,
And a resolve.
You bring me peace,
Deeper joy than I've known
So far,
And so much more
Understanding of love.
You're secure.
And I'm decidedly,
Irrevocably yours.

## A Version of Valentine

You are so many things to me:
You are present with me,
Safe, kind, and thoughtful,
Every single day
Steadily chipping away
At the callouses
Of emotional self-harm
And mini-prisons
Of self-inflicted whirlwinds,
Chaotic and grossly
Disproportionate to the situations
In which I find myself with you.
You not balking at my tearfulness,
And your not shying away from the
Redefinition of what makes up
Quality time
Makes my heart explode a thousand
small deaths,
And then quavering at the end
Of the disheveled mess we made
Making up,
I feel empowered enough
For killing zombies and bursting into laughter.
This is not a thing to put on a valentine card
But it's what makes you
My valentine,
My forever valentine,
My favorite forever valentine love.
Thank you for not seeing me as ruined

Or ruining,
But as sharp and wise and worthy.
So take this irreverent valentine poem,
And hold onto me tightly,
And we can soak in each other's goodness
And safety and love.

**Holding Space**

You hold space for me.
I wasn't sure
Before
What holding space meant.
I thought it sounded
A little bit strange
And maybe kind of
Kooky.
But there's a peace
In the chaos, in knowing
I am understood
And well-liked,
Despite my flaws.
There's an infinite marble
In the pocket of the universe,
The color of a galaxy,
Held between a whisper of magic
And an iron bed frame—
And every time I have a
Little breakdown,
It's like you can somehow
See that speck of light
And then you settle the stardust
Back into my eyes.
Holding space for a person
Is a form of love.
I'm so relieved and giddy
To have found out not only what
Someone holding space for me feels like,

But to learn how to also
Do this
For others.
Igniting the sparkles
Of the world
Is no small thing:
And you're good at it.
And I love that about you.

# About the Author

Ana Marie Shepherdson Smith is a poet living in Edmond, Oklahoma with her husband, two daughters, two dogs, and two cats. She hated writing when she was a young homeschooler, and was at risk of failing her ninth grade English class, but by her junior year in college had won an award for being an outstanding writer and went on to receive her BA in English from Sam Houston State University. She likes spending time reading, painting, getting tattooed, watching various forms of media, baking, and discussing psychology. She is learning daily that her voice is vital, and her words matter.

**_You can follow her poetry on Instagram @anamssmith_**

# Acknowledgements

**WITH DEEPEST GRATITUDE TO:**
My husband, Michael, for his unwavering dedication to my journey of self-discovery, and his steady, uplifting support from the moment we met. My eldest daughter, Rosalee, for her hugs, dance parties, camaraderie, bravery and love, and my youngest daughter, Tabitha, for her baby giggles, and mostly-calm demeanor. My sisters, Sara and Becca, for their endless bolstering, kindness, honest feedback, humor, and belief in my goodness. Colleen, whose expertise has colored my writing from the very beginning. My English professors, but especially Dr. Gene Young, because he has always believed I am an outstanding writer. Sarah, Matt, Peter, and Heather, for helping me navigate through my abuse, divorce, and put myself back together with the super glue of suggested songs, books, and media, for reading many of these poems as they were written, and for your unwavering friendship. Winter, and Laile for always letting me bounce ideas off of them, and for being strong, independent, creative, beautiful friends. Mitchell, for pushing me to write with more authenticity and courage in the midst of terrifying depression. Alexander, Gavin, James, and Valeria, for reminding me that I love creative writing. Edgar, for continuing to ask the hard questions.

# Poems Listed Alphabetically by Title

www.ingramcontent.com/pod-product-compliance
Lightning Source LLC
La Vergne TN
LVHW051426080426
835508LV00022B/3266